TWO FOR THE PRICE
OF ONE

Dicing with a Dictionary

TWO FOR THE PRICE OF ONE

Dicing with a Dictionary

Muriel Box

The Book Guild Ltd.
Sussex, England

The Book Guild Ltd.
25 High Street,
Lewes, Sussex

First published 1994
© Muriel Box 1994
Set in Palacio
Typesetting by Ashford Setting & Design Services
Ashford, Middlesex
Printed in Great Britain by
Antony Rowe Ltd,
Chippenham, Wiltshire.

A catalogue record for this book is available
from the British Library

ISBN 0 86332 713 3

CONTENTS

INTRODUCTION

In her old age, my mother, erstwhile scriptwriter and pioneer film director, became fascinated by the vagaries of the English language, especially with its many double meanings. She was intrigued by the confusion these might cause the student struggling to come to terms with this most elusive of tongues and decided to make this little book to help them.

It is in fact a personal collection of homonyms. That more definitive collections already existed she seemed blissfully unaware, devoting her waning years to this new occupation with commendable singleness of purpose. Somewhere along the way she became enthralled by her ancient *Concise Oxford Dictionary*, deferring to its authority beyond the call of common sense.

After her death we continued the preparation of her little book for publication with the seriousness due to a supplementary textbook. Her grandson, Charlie prepared a few suitable illustrations as chapter headings.

It was at this point that the whole enterprise changed character. He pointed out that what we had to deal with was not a textbook at all, but an endearing mixture of oddities. Straight-forward definitions are interspersed with undigested chunks of *Concise Oxford*, vintage 1911, served neat, which appear as delightful absurdities in this new context.

So we forbore to edit it and save for minor secretarial work it remains as she wrote it, complete with all its anomalies

7

and peculiarities. We hope that there is as much fun — and instruction — to be derived from these as from the sixty or so gentle drawings which Charlie made to go with them.

Leonora Box.

Author's Preface

Listening to English conversation can be a daunting experience for foreigners who feel confident after studying the language from textbooks or in the classroom, only to find its ambiguities can prove painful and embarrassing in certain situations.*1

There are vast numbers of words which sound the same but are spelled differently and have different meanings. There are also vast numbers of words which sound the same and are spelled the same, and yet have different meanings.

A good linguist needs to be aware of the subtleties and variations encountered when listening to spoken English which are not so evident when reading the language.

For clarification it is best to place these words into two main groups: those which have dissimilar spelling and dissimilar meaning, but sound exactly the same, and those which have the same spelling and the same sound yet entirely different meanings.

Examples of groups A and B are as follows:

Group A

SENT	*v.*	p.p. of to send: dispatched a letter, parcel etc.
SCENT	*n.*	perfume, aroma.
CENT	*n.*	small coin in American and other currencies.

GROUP B

POUND	*n.*	coin in English currency. Weight equal to 16oz.
	v.	to bring heavy pressure to bear on an object.
	n.	an enclosure for prisoners.

These two groups together formed a large collection of well over 3,500 words, a formidable number for any foreigner to memorize and learn their meanings. So a certain number were not included since to do so would have defeated the purpose of the book, which is to provide quick and easy access to answers to particular questions. To produce a slim volume for consultation during a conversation is preferable to carrying a weighty and cumbersome dictionary in such circumstances. To extract the right meaning from a word which has a dozen or more interpretations takes a considerable time. When the correct word has been found the conversation may have moved on and the foreigner find that he has lost the drift of it.

A number of twin-sounding words have been omitted for a special reason. They are those which, on examination, were considered to be insufficiently contradictory. These occur mainly in the B group, have the same spelling, are identical in sound, but lack the qualities that make them entirely different. To illustrate, the following twin-words, although they are spelt the same and sound the same, show a difference in meaning which is not sharp enough. Their only difference lies in the fact that one is a noun and the other a verb.

BOAST	*n.*	vainglorious statement, self-exaltation.
BOAST	*v.*	to extol oneself, to brag.

Pronunciation can also alter the interpretation of some words, for example, where the same word spelled in the same way changes its meaning when the sound is changed.

10

The word 'tear' when pronounced 'teer' means a drop of liquid from the eye, but when pronounced 'tare' it means to split apart, to sunder. Similarly 'read' in the present tense sounds like 'reed' while in the past tense it sounds like 'red'.[*2]

Muriel Box

Footnotes:

[*1.] In order to keep down the size of the book, we decided to leave out group B and only include words spelled differently. In fact this is not such a great loss, since the greater number of those in the second group are not really different words, coincidentally spelled the same, but natural growths away from the same root. The final paragraph of my mother's introduction shows some intimation of this on her part.

[*2.] This last paragraph suggests a whole new field of operations. Alas it was never embarked upon.

[*] (MB) put her own footnote here as follows:

'A foreign delegate rose in an international conference to declare during his speech that "members were firmly holding on to their long standing fallacies, refusing to relinquish them ..."

Suddenly to his surprise, a guffaw of laughter broke from one of the English delegates, followed by another, and then a third. Soon the entire gathering which had hitherto been a staid and rather sleepy affair, became distinctly hilarious.

The speaker, failing to realize his allusion to 'fallacies' could be interpreted as 'phalluses', was quite bewildered by the unusual response.'

EDITOR'S NOTES

Each pair of words is listed alphabetically so that the ones with the initial letters nearest A will come first and be listed first. Where a pair starts with different initial letters they will be listed under both, with a definition only in the slot nearest the beginning of the alphabet, the only exceptions to this being some of those which are illustrated. These have been distributed as evenly as possible throughout the book so that sometimes the later initial is favoured.

Most of the words have more than one form, being often both nouns and verbs. We have generally favoured the noun form where there was a choice.

My mother held no truck with phonetic alphabets, so I am afraid there is no pronunciation guide — save that all the pairs sound the same. If you get one wrong, you'll get them both wrong!

Abbreviations are as follows:

n.	noun	coll.	colloquial
v.	verb	pro.	pronoun
p.p.	past participle	arch.	archaic
pl.	plural	prep.	preposition
a.	adjective	esp.	especially
adv.	adverb	e.g.	for example
conj.	conjunction	met.	metaphorical
pre.	prefix	p.	past tense
int.	interjection	fig.	figuratively

A

After much ale he ailed.

AIL	*v.*	to be ill or upset.
ALE	*n.*	fermented drink, like beer.
AIR	*see*	HEIR
AISLE	*n.*	division or passage in a church; one divided from nave by pillar.
ISLE	*n.*	small island (poetic).

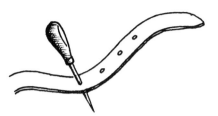

That's all there is to an awl.

| ALL | *n.* | the whole quantity, amount or extent of something. |
| AWL | *n.* | small tool with a slender tapering blade used by shoemakers for piercing holes in leather. |

"You are not allowed to speak aloud."

ALLOWED	*v.*	p.p. of to allow: permitted to act in a certain manner or circumstance.
ALOUD	*adv.*	sound palpably heard; opposite to whispered.
ALMS	*n.pl.*	charitable donations; gifts to the poor.
ARMS	*n.pl.*	weapons; the upper limbs of the body.

He swiftly altered the altar

ALTAR   *n.*   flat-topped table or block used for religious services.

ALTER   *v.*   to change the character of people or things.

17

He was anti raising the ante.

ANTE	*n.coll.*	stake made by poker player.
ANTI	*pre.*	against, in opposition to, rivalling.
ARC	*n.*	curve, part of the circumference of a circle.
ARK	*n.*	chest for religious ceremony; old type of vessel, i.e. Noah's Ark.
ASCENT	*n.*	act of rising; moving up a slope, steps or lift.
ASSENT	*n.*	expression of agreement or consent.
ATE	*see*	EIGHT
AUGER	*n.*	a tool for boring holes in wood.
AUGUR	*n.*	a Roman religious official who foretold events by omens derived from the actions of birds; a soothsayer.

| AUGHT | *n.* | opposite of nought. |
| OUGHT | *v.* | to be bound; under an obligation. |

| AURAL | *see* | ORAL |

| AWE | *see* | OAR |

| AYE | *see* | EYE |

An ark on an arc.

B

BAA   *n.*   the bleating note of a lamb.
BAR   *n.*   barrier; counter in an inn.

A baa bar.

BADE	*v.*	p.p. of to bid: ordered or commanded.
BAYED	*v.*	p.p. of to bay: barked or howled, as a large dog.
BAIL	*n.*	security given for prisoner pending trial which gives him temporary release.
BALE	*n.*	package of merchandise, hay or straw.
	n.	woe; pain; misery (poetic).
BAIZE	*n.*	Coarse woolen stuff with long nap used for covering tables.
BAYS	*n.pl.*	part of the sea filling wide-mouthed inlets in a coastline.

"Mmm..... baize bays."

BALD	*a.*	partially or wholly hairless.
BAWLED	*v.*	p.p. of to bawl: shouted in a loud tone.
BALL	*n.*	solid or hollow sphere, particularly as used in games.
BAWL	*v.*	shout or speak in a noisy way.
BALM	*n.*	fragrant and medicinal exudation from certain trees; ointment, salve.
BARM	*n.*	froth on fermenting malt liquor; yeast; leaven.
BALMY	*a.*	gentle, fragrant, soothing, perfumed, soft.
BARMY	*a.coll.*	loony or soft in the head; a little mad.
BAND	*n.*	company of armed men; body of musicians; flat thin strip of material like a ribbon.
BANNED	*v.*	p.p. of to ban: prohibited, interdicted, outlawed, cursed.
BARD	*n.*	Celtic Minstrel; early poet.
BARRED	*v.*	p.p. of to bar: kept out; obstructed.
BARE	*a.*	unclothed, undisguised, unadorned, scanty.
BEAR	*n.*	heavy, partly carnivorous, thick furred quadruped.
	v.	carry.
BARK	*n.*	skin or outer sheath of a tree trunk; normal sharp cry of a dog.
BARQUE	*n.*	three-masted vessel with fore and main masts square-rigged.

BARON	n.	peer; one with honourable service summoned to Parliament.
BARREN	a.	incapable of bearing children, fruit or produce.
BASE	a.	morally low; menial; cowardly; despicable.
BASS	n.	lowest male voice.
BASED	v.	p.p. of to base: supported on a foundation; established.
BASTE	v.	moisten roasting meat with fat to prevent burning.
BATON	n.	staff of office; musical conductor's wand for beating time.
BATTEN	n.	narrow piece of timber used for strength or fixing, as in 'batten down the hatches' (nautical).
BAY	n.	broad inlet in a coastline.
BEY	n.	Turkish ruler or governor.
BEACH	n.	sea shore covered with sand or pebbles.
BEECH	n.	smooth-barked, glossy-leaved, mast-bearing forest tree; white breasted marten found in Southern Europe.
BEAN	n.	kind of leguminous plant bearing kidney-shaped seeds in long pods, as the coffee bean.
BEEN	v.	p.p. of to be: as in 'I've *been* up to London to look at the Queen'.
BEAT	v.	strike repeatedly; surpass; overcome.
BEET	n.	plant with succulent root.

BEER	*n.*	alcoholic liquor made from fermented malt flavoured with hops.
BIER	*n.*	movable stand on which a coffin is taken to the grave.
BERRY	*n.*	any small rounded juicy fruit without a stone.
BURY	*v.*	deposit in, commit to the earth; perform burial rites.
BERTH	*n.*	place for ship to swing at anchor; convenient ship's room.
BIRTH	*n.*	bringing forth of offspring; origin; beginning; parentage.

A bite shaped bight.

BIGHT	*n.*	recess of coast; bay; loop of rope.
BITE	*v.*	cut into or nip with the teeth; snap off; grip.
BILLED	*v.*	p.p. of to bill: announced publicly on a bill; drafted Act of Parliament.
BUILD	*n.*	style of construction; make; proportions of human body.

BLEW	*v.*	p. blow: made the air move.
BLUE	*a.*	colour, like the sky or bluebells.
BOAR	*n.*	male pig.
BORE	*n.*	tidal wave with precipitous front moving up some estuaries.
BOARD	*n.*	stated meals provided at fixed rate for lodger.
	v.	force one's way on board ship.
BORED	*v.*	p.p. of to bore: wearied by tedious talk or dullness.
BOLD	*a.*	courageous; enterprising; confident; vigorous.
BOWLED	*v.*	p.p. of to bowl: delivered a ball, as in cricket.
BOLDER	*a.*	more courageous and confident than another.
BOULDER	*n.*	large erratic block of weather-beaten stone.
BOOS	*n.pl.*	sounds of disapproval; hoots at speaker.
BOOZE	*v.coll.*	drink deeply; go on a drinking bout.
BORN	*v.*	p.p. of to bear: came into the world by birth.
BOURN	*n.*	limit; 'the vndiscouered Countrey from whose Borne No Trauller returnes.' Hamlet III. i. 79.
	n.	small stream.
BOUGH	*n.*	tree branch.
BOW	*v.*	submit to the inevitable; bend or kneel in submission.

| BOY | *n.* | male child till puberty, loosely till the age of nineteen or twenty. |
| BUOY | *n.* | anchored float showing navigable course, or reefs. |

A boy on a buoy.

BRAKE	*n.*	device for stopping a wheel, car or train.
BREAK	*v.*	separate into parts without cutting;
	n.	points scored continuously in billiards.
BREAD	*n.*	food made from flour moistened, kneaded and baked.
BRED	*v.*	p.p. of to breed: with 'well', coming from good stock, race or strain; having fine hereditary qualities.

Bred to bake bread ..... (see KNEAD).

BRIDAL	*a.*	for a wedding.
BRIDLE	*n.*	head gear or harness for a horse, including headstall, bit and rein.
BROACH	*v.*	veer or cause a ship to veer and present its side to the windward waves.
BROOCH	*n.*	ornamental jewelled safety-pin for fastening parts of female dress.
BUT	*n.*	an objection.
BUTT	*n.*	wine or ale cask; any barrel; object of ridicule; target.
BUYER	*n.*	someone who obtains goods for payment; agent who selects and purchases stock for a large shop.
BYRE	*n.*	cowhouse.

C

CACHE   *n.*   hiding place for treasure, provisions or ammunition.

CASH   *v.*   give or obtain ready money for cheque or note; 'cash in': die. (coll.)

CADDIE   *n.*   golf player's attendant for carrying clubs etc.

CADDY   *n.*   small box for holding tea.

The caddie brought the caddy ..... (see TEA)

CANNON	*n.*	heavy mounted gun.
CANON	*n.*	an ecclesiastical law; list of books permitted by the church; member of cathedral chapter.
CANTER	*n.*	easy gallop; at the pace of the Canterbury pilgrims.
CANTOR	*n.*	singer whose duty is to lead the singing in church.
CANVAS	*n.*	strong unbleached cloth of hemp or flax for sails, tents or tapestry.
CANVASS	*n.*	discuss thoroughly; solicit votes from constituency.
CARAT	*n.*	measure of weight for precious stones, about 3½ grains.
CARROT	*n.*	plant with tapering orange-coloured edible root.
CAUGHT	*v.*	p.p. of to catch: captured, ensnared.
COURT	*n.*	space enclosed by walls or buildings.
	v.	pay court to: make love to.
CAULK	*v.*	stop up seams of ship with melted pitch and oakum.
CORK	*n.*	bark of cork oak tree; bottle stopper made of this.
CAUSE	*n.*	origin or agent of something; motive for action.
CORES	*n.*	pl. of core, see below.

"Caw! What a core!"

CAW	*n.*	cry of a crow, raven or rook.
CORE	*n.*	centre section in fruit containing seeds encased in tough sharp skin.
CEDE	*v.*	relinquish, grant, surrender.
SEED	*n.*	flowering plant's germ of reproduction.
CELL	*see*	SELL.
CELLAR	*n.*	underground room for storage; wine so kept.
SELLER	*n.*	one who exchanges goods for money.
CENSER	*n.*	vessel in which incense is burned.
CENSOR	*n.*	official who licenses or suppresses books, plays, films, news or military intelligence.
CENT	*n.*	a hundred cents or small coins which make up an American or other dollar.
SCENT	*n.*	odour of agreeable kind; perfume.
SENT	*v.*	p.p. of to send: despatched letters, parcels, messenger etc.

CHASED	*v.*	p.p. of to chase: hunted; pursued.
CHASTE	*a.*	pure, virgin, abstaining from sexual activity.
CHEAP	*a.*	inexpensive, worthless, of little account, easily got.
CHEEP	*n.*	shrill, feeble note as of a young bird.
CHILLI	*n.*	dried pod of capsicum, used as relish or made into cayenne pepper.
CHILLY	*a.*	rather cold; not genial.
CHOIR	*n.*	group of singers performing musical parts of a church service.
QUIRE	*n.*	measure of paper; four sheets folded to form eight leaves.
CHORD	*n.*	group of notes sounded together, combined together according to some harmonic system.
CORD	*n.*	thin rope; thick string; ribbed fabric like corduroy.
CITE	*n.*	mention as an example, quote in support of argument.
SIGHT	*n.*	faculty of vision.
SITE	*n.*	ground on which a town or building stood, stands or is to stand.
CLAUSE	*n.*	part of a sentence; single proviso to treaty, law or contract.
CLAWS	*n.pl.*	pointed horny nails of a bird or beast's foot.
CLIMB	*v.*	ascend, mount or go up.
CLIME	*n.*	climate as metaphor for region, country or area (poetic).

31

COAL	*n.*	hard black mineral of carbonized vegetable matter found below the earth's surface and mined for fuel.
KOHL	*n.*	powder, usually antimony, used in the East to darken eyelids.
COARSE	*a.*	common, inferior, rough in texture.
COURSE	*n.*	direction planned, path taken, ground for races.
COIN	*n.*	rounded piece of metal forming money by bearing official stamp.
QUOIN	*n.*	corner-stone of a building.
COLONEL	*n.*	highest officer in an army regiment.
KERNEL	*n.*	soft edible part within the hard shell of a nut or stone of fruit.
COPS	*n.pl.coll.*	policemen.
COPSE	*n.*	underwood; ground covered with trees to form a coppice.

Cops in the copse.

CREAK	*n.*	modified squeak or scraping sound made by hinges lacking oil, or new boots in first use.
CREEK	*n.*	narrow outlet of river to the sea.
CREWS	*n.pl.*	whole bodies of men manning ship or boat; gang; company; set; mob.
CRUISE	*n.*	a cruising voyage for pleasure at less than top speed.
CUE	*see*	QUEUE
CURB	*n.*	strap pulled under jaw of horse as check or restraint.
KERB	*n.*	edge of a pavement or path which lines a street.
CURD	*n.*	cheese or junket made by the action of acids on milk.
KURD	*n.*	native of Kurdistan.
CURRANT	*n.*	dried fruit of a seedless variety of grapes grown in the Levant.
CURRENT	*n.*	running stream of water, air, electricity moving in one direction.

D

DAM	*n.*	barrier constructed to hold back water and raise its level.
DAMN	*v.*	condemn; censure; curse; secure withdrawal of a play.
DAYS	*n.pl.*	times while the sun is above the horizon, opposite to nights.
DAZE	*v.*	stupify, dazzle, bewilder.
DEAR	*a.*	term of affection, used as usual form of address in letters; precious, highly-priced, costly.
DEER	*n.*	kinds of ruminant quadruped with deciduous branching horns.

"Dear Deer,"

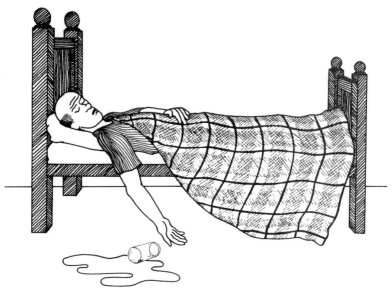

Much diseased, he deceased.

DECEASED	*v.*	p.p. of to decease: dead; departed.
DISEASED	*a.*	affected with disease, morbid, depraved.
DENSE	*a.*	closely compacted; crowded together; stupid, crass.
DENTS	*n.pl.*	surface marks; impressions from blows of a sharp instrument.
DEPOSE	*v.*	remove from office, dethrone.
DEPOTS	*n.pl.*	store houses; headquarters of a regiment.
DESCENT	*n.*	descending motion; the way down; decline.
DISSENT	*n.*	difference of opinion; refusal to give assent.

35

DESERT	*n.*	uninhabited, barren, waterless region.
DESSERT	*n.*	course of fruit, sweetmeats etc. at the end of dinner.
DEW	*n.*	atmospheric vapour condensed in small drops on cool surfaces between evening and morning.
DUE	*n.*	person's right; what is owed to them; owing; debt.
DIE	*v.*	cease to live; expire from many causes.
	n.	small cube numbered with spots for games, usually pl.: dice.
DYE	*n.*	colour produced by dyeing; tinge; hue.
DIRE	*a.*	dreadful, calamitous.
DYER	*n.*	one who dyes cloth etc.
DISCUS	*n.*	heavy disc thrown in ancient Greek and modern Olympic games.
DISCUSS	*v.*	examine by argument; debate.

Discuss the discus.

DOE	*n.*	female of fallow deer, hare, rabbit.
DOUGH	*n.*	bread paste, kneaded ready for baking; money (coll.)
DOER	*n.*	one who performs, acts, deals with things, works actively.
DOUR	*a.*	severe, stern, obstinate.
DOES	*n.pl.*	plural of doe.
DOZE	*n.*	half-sleep, drowse, short slumber.
DOLLAR	*n.*	unit of US and other currency.
DOLOUR	*n.*	sorrow, distress (poetic).
DONE	*n.*	p.p. of to do: accomplished, completed; swindled (coll.).
DUN	*a.*	greyish brown colour as of a mouse.
DUAL	*a.*	two; double in character.
DUEL	*n.*	fight by appointment in front of witnesses with lethal weapons to settle a dispute between individuals.

E

EARN   *v.*   obtain as a reward of labour or merit.
URN   *n.*   special vase for storing the ashes of the dead; a vessel or measure.

EIGHT   *n.*   number in excess of seven by one.
ATE   *v.*   p. of to eat: took food, nourishment.

"He just ate eight courses."

EWE	*see*	YEW
EWES	*see*	USE

EYE	*n.*	organ of sight, what you see with.
AYE	*int.*	coll. form of 'yes'.
	adv.	ever, always (arch.)

"I looked him in the eye and said "Aye"."

F

FAINT	v.	become utterly insensible; lose courage.
FEINT	n.	sham attack, thrust or military assault;
	v.	simulate; pretend.

| FAIR | a. | beautiful; blond; just; unbiased; legitimate. |
| FARE | n. | cost of traveller's conveyance; food; provisions. |

| FALLACIES n.pl. | | misleading arguments; sophisms; delusions; errors. |
| PHALLUSES n.pl. | | images of the penis venerated in religions as symbols of the generative power in nature. |

| FARTHER | a.adv. | at a more advanced point, greater extent or distance; additional. |
| FATHER | n. | male parent. |

| FATE | n. | power determining events, destiny, appointed lot. |
| FÊTE | n. | festival, great entertainment. |

| FAUN | n. | one of Latin rural deities, with horns and tail. |
| FAWN | n. | young fallow deer; show of affection by tail wagging. |

| FEAT | n. | noteworthy act; deed of valour; surprising trick. |
| FEET | n. | pl. of foot: termination of legs beginning at the ankles. |

"Phew! Thank God there's only a few!"

| FEW | a. | not many, no great number. |
| PHEW | int. | exclamation of surprise or disgust. |

| FILE | n. | kind of appliance for holding papers arranged for reference. |
| PHIAL | n. | small glass bottle especially for liquid medicine. (Also see VIAL, VILE and VIOL). |

| FILTER | n. | contrivance for freeing liquids from suspended impurities by passing them through sand or charcoal or paper etc. |
| PHILTRE | n. | love potion. |

| FIND | v. | come across; fall in with; light upon; discover. |
| FINED | v. | p.p. of to fine: made to pay money for an offence. |

41

It was then he discovered the flaw in his floor.

| FLAW | *n.* | crack; breach; rent; imperfection; blemish. |
| FLOOR | *n.* | lower surface of a room; bottom of sea, cave etc.; part of Houses of Parliament where members speak. |

| FLOCKS | *n.pl.* | large numbers of animals of one kind, especially birds or sheep. |
| PHLOX | *n.* | genus of plant with large clusters of salver-shaped flowers in many colours. |

| FLOE | *n.* | sheet of floating ice. |
| FLOW | *v.* | glide along, as a stream; circulate; undulate; literary style. |

42

FOALED	*v.*	p.p. of to foal: gave birth to a young colt or filly.
FOLD	*n.*	thing doubled over on itself; enclosure for sheep.

"To make things simpler three will now stand for four."

FOR	*prep., conj.*	instead of; in favour of — as opposed to 'against'; with the purpose of; on account of — and many many more.
FORE	*a.*	in front or before.
FOUR	*n.*	one more than three.
FISHER	*n.*	fisherman, angler; one who catches fish.
FISSURE	*n.*	cleft made by the splitting or separating of parts; cleavage.
FIZZ	*n.*	a hissing, spluttering, bubbling sound.
PHIZ	*n.*	face, features of a person (abbr. physiognomy) (coll.)
FLAIR	*n.*	selective instinct for what is excellent.
FLARE	*n.*	sudden burst of flame; signal rocket.

43

FOREGO	*v.*	precede in time; decide before e.g. 'a foregone conclusion'.
FORGO	*v.*	abstain from; go without; relinquish.
FORT	*n.*	fortified place; castle or fortified trading station.
FOUGHT	*v.*	p. tense of fight: was actively engaged in fighting.
FORTH	*adv., prep.*	forwards; coming out into view; forwards in time.
FOURTH	*n.*	next after third: Fourth of July Anniversary of US Independence.
FOUL	*a.*	offensive to the senses; loathsome, stinking, dirty, soiled.
FOWL	*n.*	birds eaten for their flesh as food.
FRANC	*n.*	unit of French currency.
FRANK	*a.*	open, candid, outspoken, ingenuous.
	n.	postmark for cancelling stamps.
FREES	*v.*	sets at liberty; emancipates; rids of domination.
FREEZE	*v.*	be converted into, or covered with ice; refrigerate; stop all movement.
FRIEZE	*n.*	kind of coarse woolen cloth with nap on one side only.
FRIAR	*n.*	member of certain religious orders.
FRYER	*n.*	person who engages in frying, esp. fish, potatoes etc.

G

GAFF   *n.*   barbed fishing spear or stick with iron hook for landing large fish.

GAFFE   *n.*   blunder, indiscrete remark or act, *faux pas*.

Gaffe with a gaff.

GAGE	*n.*	pledge deposited as security e.g. glove thrown down in a challenge to fight.
	n.	type of fruit as damson, greengage.
GUAGE	*n.*	standard or measure to which things must conform.
GAIT	*n.*	manner of walking; bearing or carriage.
GATE	*n.*	opening in wall of city or enclosure made for entrance and exit and capable of being closed with a barrier.
GEEZER	*n.*	old person, old creature (coll.)
GEYSER	*n.*	intermittent hot spring throwing up a column of hot water; apparatus for heating water.
GILD	*v.*	cover with a thin layer of gold leaf or otherwise soften down an unpleasant necessity.
GUILD	*n.*	society for mutual aid, esp. mediaeval fellowships of craftsmen.
GILT	*n.*	thin covering of gold, in book binding used for tooling letters of gold.
GUILT	*n.*	the fact or state of having done wrong or committed an offence.
GIN	*see*	JINN
GNAW	*v.*	bite persistently and wear away thus; corrode.
NOR	*conj.*	neither; and not.
GORILLA	*n.*	large powerful ferocious anthropoid ape.
GUERILLA	*n.*	soldier engaged in irregular war waged by small bands acting independently.

"There you are — one gramme of gram."

GRAM	*n.*	chick-pea or any pulse used as fodder.
GRAMME	*n.*	unit of weight in the metric system.
GRATE	*n.*	frame of metal bars for containing fuel in a fireplace.
	v.	to reduce to small particles by rubbing on a rough surface e.g. grated cheese.
GREAT	*a.*	large, big, important, elevated beyond the ordinary.

GREASE	*n.*	fat of deer or other game; melted fat of dead animals; lubrication.
GREECE	*n.*	Hellenic country.
GRISLY	*a.*	causing horror, terror or superstitious dread.
GRIZZLY	*n.*	grey, greyish, grey-haired.
GROAN	*n.*	deep inarticulate sound expressing pain or grief.
GROWN	*v.*	p.p. of to grow: fully developed, sprouted, germinated, got larger.
GUESSED	*v.*	p.p. of to guess: estimated without measurement; hazarded an opinion about solution to riddle or problem.
GUEST	*n.*	person entertained at another's house or table.
GUIDE	*v.*	one who shows the way; conductor of travellers or tourists.
GUYED	*v.*	p.p. of to guy: ridiculed, 'sent up' in fun.
GUISE	*n.*	style of attire; garb; external appearance; semblance; pretence.
GUYS	*n.pl.*	ropes or chains used to steady a crane or tent.
	n.pl.	men (US) (coll.).

H

HAIL	*n.*	pellets of ice falling in a shower or storm; shower of missiles, curses.
HALE	*a.*	robust, vigorous, esp. of old persons.
HALL	*n.*	large public room or building; entrance room in a house.
HAUL	*v.*	pull; drag forcibly; gather in.
HANGAR	*n.*	large shed for housing aeroplanes or machinery.
HANGER	*n.*	loop, catch or frame on which something is hung.
	n.	wooded slope of a hill.
HART	*n.*	male of the red deer when adult.
HEART	*n.*	hollow organ keeping up the circulation of blood, by contracting and dilating.
HAW	*n.*	fruit of the hawthorne tree.
HOAR	*a.*	white, greyish as in 'hoarfrost' or 'hoary beard'.
WHORE	*n.*	prostitute or strumpet.
HAY	*n.*	long grass mown and dried for fodder.
HEY	*int.*	expression of enquiry, surprise.
	n.	country dance.

49

"He'll heal your heel."

HEAL	*v.*	restore a person to health; cure someone of disease, become sound.
HEEL	*n.*	hinder part of human foot below ankle.
HE'LL	*n. & v.*	abbreviation of 'he will'.
HEAR	*v.*	perceive sound with the ear.
HERE	*adv.*	in this place, as opposed to 'there'; at this point in the discourse.

"You can hear it from here."

HEARD   *v.*   p.p. of to hear: received sound; noticed sounds.

HERD   *n.*   company of animals or cattle feeding and travelling together.

"He says he thought he heard a herd."

HEIR	*n.*	one legally entitled to inherit property from another.
AIR	*n.*	gaseous atmosphere breathed by all living things.
	n.	melody, song.

The heir heard an air in the air.

| HEROIN | *n.* | addictive drug prepared from morphine. |
| HEROINE | *n.* | demigoddess; heroic woman; chief woman in a novel, play or film etc. |

HEW	*v.*	chop a thing to pieces with an axe or sword; cut into shape.
HUE	*n.*	colour, tint or complexion.
	n.	clamour of pursuit; outcry.

| HI! | *int.* | call of attention-seeking; greeting. |
| HIGH | *a. adv.* | far up; aloft; of great upward extent. |

| HIGHER | *adv.* | situated further above the ground; of greater rank. |
| HIRE | *n.* | payment by contract for use of a thing or for a personal service. |

| HIM | *pro.* | referring to a male person or animal. |
| HYMN | *n.* | song of praise to God. |

HOARSE	*a.*	rough, husky, croaking — of a voice.
HORSE	*n.*	solid-hoofed quadruped with flowing mane and tail used as a beast of burden and for riding.
HOARD	*n.*	stock or store laid by; a mass of money; overstock of food.
HORDE	*n.*	great troop of Tartars or other nomads; large number of people.
HO!	*int.*	exclaimation of surprise, admiration or triumph.
HOE	*n.*	garden tool for loosening the soil or scraping up weeds.
HOLE	*n.*	hollow place in a solid body; cavity for a ball in games, e.g. golf.
WHOLE	*a.*	in a sound condition; uninjured; not broken; intact; complete.
HOLEY	*a.*	full of holes.
HOLY	*a.*	sacred, spiritually perfect.
WHOLLY	*a.*	entirely, exclusively.
HOUR	*n.*	measure of time: sixty minutes; one twenty-fourth of a day.
OUR	*a.*	of or belonging to us; that we are associated with.

I

IDLE	*a.*	unoccupied; lazy; ineffective; indolent.
IDOL	*n.*	image of deity used as object of worship; false god.
IN	*prep.*	expressing inclusion or position within limits of space, time or circumstance.
INN	*n.*	public house; house for lodging etc. of travellers.
ION	*n.*	an electrically charged particle or atom.
IRON	*n.*	metal, largely used for tools; tool for smoothing out linen.
ISLE	*see*	AISLE

"You'll find them all in the inn ....."

J

JAM	*n.*	sweet spread for bread or cakes etc.; blockage e.g. *traffic jam*.
JAMB	*n.*	side post of a door or window.
JINKS	*n.pl.*	boisterous sports; merry making.
JINX	*n.*	person or thing bringing bad luck.
JINN	*n.*	in Mohammedan demonology a spirit lower than the angels able to appear in human form.
GIN	*n.*	intoxicating spirit distilled from grain.

..... even the jinn drinking gin."

K

KERB	*see*	CURB
KERNEL	*see*	COLONEL
KEY	*n.*	instrument for moving the bolt of a lock forwards or backwards hence unlocking it.
QUAY	*n.*	solid stationary artificial landing place lying alongside or projecting into the water, for unloading, mooring, ships.
KHOL	*see*	COAL
KNAVE	*see*	NAVE
KNEAD	*v.*	to press and roll dough for making bread or damp clay in making pottery.
NEED	*n.*	a want; necessity to take a course of action; possible obligation to act as required.

..... because they need to knead. (see BREAD)

56

KNEW	*v.*	p.p. of to know: to have been acquainted with; understood; been aware of a fact.
NEW	*a.*	fresh; novel; of recent origin; not yet used.
KNIGHT	*see*	NIGHT.
KNIT	*v.*	by using needles and yarn of various textures to make fine patterns in garments by hand.
NIT	*n.*	egg of a parasitic insect found on humans.
KNOB	*n.*	rounded projection from a hard surface such as the handle of a door; a small lump of sugar.
NOB	*n.*	member of the upper classes; your head; Jack in cribbage (coll.).
KNOT	*see*	NOT
KNOW	*v.*	recognize; identify; be acquainted with; be aware of.
NO	*n.a.*	negative response; not any; not at all; a denial, refusal.
KNOWS	*v.*	third person singular form of to know.
NOSE	*n.*	member of the head or face placed above the mouth containing nostrils and serving as the organ of smell.
KURD	*see*	CURD

L

LACKS	*v.*	wants, needs, is without, is deficient in.
LAX	*a.*	loose, relaxed, negligent, careless, not strict, vague, porous.
LADE	*v.*	put cargo on board ship; carry goods as cargo: ship's 'bill of lading'.
LAID	*v.*	p.p. of to lay: prostrated; put down; settled; put forward a claim.

"He's lain in the lane since closing time last night."

LAIN	*v.*	p.p. of to lie: had one's body in a more or less horizontal position on the ground.
LANE	*n.*	narrow road, usually between hedges; narrow street or passage.
LAM	*v.*	to thrash; hit hard with a cane.
LAMB	*n.*	young of a sheep.

Lama on a llama.

LAMA	*n.*	Tibetan or Mongolian Buddhist monk.
LLAMA	*n.*	South American ruminant allied to the camel, but smaller, humpless and wooly-haired.
LAPPS	*n.pl.*	northern race of people from Lapland.
LAPS	*n.pl.*	circuits of a race track.
	n.pl.	place from waist to knees which when level can be used for nursing infant.
LAPSE	*n.*	slight mistake in speech or conduct; slip of the pen; failing to continue through want of vigour.
LAUD	*n.*	hymn of praise; celebration.
LORD	*n.*	nobleman; peer of the realm; God.
LAWN	*n.*	glade; grass covered land; close mown turf.
	n.	kind of fine linen esp. used for bishop's sleeves.
LORN	*a.*	desolate; folorn.

LAYS	*n.*	lyrical poems intended to be sung: *Lays of Ancient Rome*.
LAZE	*v.*	be indolent, idle; pass the time away.
LEA	*n.*	tract of open ground, esp. grassland.
LEE	*n.*	shelter given by neighbouring object; the side away from the prevailing wind.
LEACH	*v.*	make liquid percolate through some material; purge matter away.
LEECH	*n.*	kind of aquatic blood-sucking worm used medically for bleeding; met. a person who sucks profit out of others.
LEAD	*n.*	heavy, easily fusible, soft, malleable metal of a dull colour.
LED	*v.*	p.p. of to lead: forced to go with one; conducted; guided by someone going in front.
LEAF	*n.*	expanded organ, usually green, of a plant, springing from the side of the stem or direct from the root.
	n.	single thickness of paper as from a book.
LIEF	*adv.*	gladly; willingly.
LEAK	*n.*	hole caused by injury or wear through which fluid makes a way out.
LEEK	*n.*	culinary herb like an onion, but without the spherical bulb; Welsh emblem.
LEANT	*v.*	p.p. of to lean: inclined e.g. leant one's body against something for support.
LENT	*v.*	p.p. of to lend: let out money on the understanding that it is returned.

60

LEASED	v.	p.p. of to lease: contracted with a lessor for rent; conveyed land or tenement to lessee for a specified time.
LEAST	a.	smallest; slightest.

A lesson in how to lessen.

LESSEN	v.	decrease; diminish.
LESSON	n.	one of the two readings from the Old and New Testament at morning or evening prayers; thing to be learned by pupil.
LESSER	adj.	not so great as the other or as the rest; minor.
LESSOR	n.	person who lets property on a lease.
LEVEE	n.	reception for visitors held on rising from bed.
LEVY	n.	collection of tax; enrolling of men for war.
LIAR	n.	teller, habitually of lies or untruths.
LYRE	n.	obsolete instrument of the harp kind, of a size for holding in the left hand, with strings, chiefly used for accompanying voice.

| LIE | *n.* | intentional false statement. |
| LYE | *n.* | water alkalised by lixiviation of vegetable ashes. |

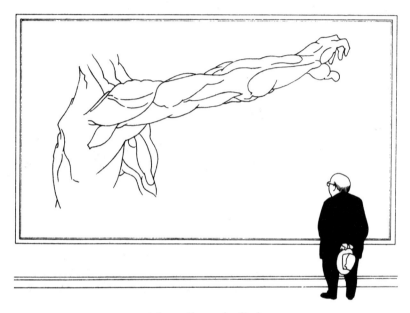

A large limn of a limb.

LIMB	*n.*	leg, arm or wing; main branch of a tree.
LIMN	*n.*	depiction; portrayal; picture.
LINKS	*n.pl.*	undulating sandy ground near seashore with turf and short grass on which golf is played.
LYNX	*n.*	animal of the cat tribe with tufted ears.
LO!	*int.*	look!; see!; behold!; jocular introduction of surprising fact.
LOW	*n.*	cry uttered forth by a cow.
	a.	opposite to high.

LOAD	*n.*	what is to be carried; burden.
LODE	*n.*	water course, open drain in fens; vein of metal ore; Pole Star.

"Well, just call it a lone loan."

LOAN	*n.*	thing or sum of money lent, to be returned with or without interest.
LONE	*a.*	solitary; companionless; isolated; unfrequented.
LOOT	*n.*	goods taken from the enemy; spoil; booty; illicit gains made by official.
LUTE	*n.*	a guitar-like instrument used from the fourteenth to seventeenth centuries.
LUMBAR	*a.*	artery, vein, nerve or vertebra of the loin.
LUMBER	*n.*	useless or cumbersome material; superfluous fat; roughly prepared timber.

M

MADE   *v.*   p.p. of to make: constructed; prepared food; brought or caused to exist.

MAID   *n.*   spinster; unmarried girl; female servant; lady attending on queen or other royalty.

..... so they made the maid.

MAGNATE	*n.*	great wealthy or eminent man.
MAGNET	*n.*	piece of iron or ore having the properties of attracting iron and of pointing north and south when suspended; something that attracts.
MAIL	*n.*	armour worn to protect the body; letters conveyed by post.
MALE	*n.*	the sex which begets offspring or performs the fecundating function; quality of being masculine.
MAIN	*n.*	principal channel or duct for water.
MANE	*n.*	long hair on neck of a horse or lion.
MAIZE	*n.*	Indian corn, and its grain.
MAZE	*n.*	complex network of paths; labyrinth; confused mass.
MANNA	*n.*	substance supplied as food to Israelites; spiritual nourishment; sweet juice from manna ash used as a gentle laxative.
MANNER	*n.*	way a thing is done, or happens.
MANOR	*n.*	English territorial unit, originally feudal, now consisting of lord's demesne and lands from which are extracted certain fees.
MARE	*n.*	female of equine animal, esp. horse.
MAYOR	*n.*	head of municipal corporation of city or borough.
MARSHAL	*n.*	officer of highest rank in some foreign armies.
MARTIAL	*a.*	of, suitable for, appropriate to warfare; brave; fond of fighting.

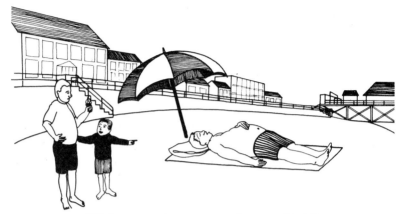
"He's got even more maw than you Dad."

MAW	*n.*	stomach; last of ruminant's four stomachs.
MORE	*n.*	greater quantity or number.
MEAN	*a.*	equally far from two extremes; not imposing in appearance; poor.
MIEN	*n.*	air or bearing of a person, as showing character or mood.
MEAT	*n.*	animal flesh as food.
MEET	*n.*	meeting of hounds and men for hunt or of cyclists.
MEDDLER	*n.*	one who busies himself unduly in the affairs of others, who interferes.
MEDLAR	*n.*	tree with fruit like small brown apple, eaten when decayed.
METAL	*n.*	any of a class of substances represented by gold, silver, copper, lead and tin etc.
METTLE	*n.*	quality of disposition; natural ardour; spirit; courage.

66

| MEWS | *n.* | set of stabling round open yard. |
| MUSE | *n.* | fit of abstraction. |

| MIGHT | *n.* | great bodily or mental strength; power to enforce one's will. |
| MITE | *n.* | small arachnid found in cheese. |

A mite of great might ..... might be dangerous.'

| MIND | *v.* | give heed to; concern oneself; take comfort. |
| MINED | *v.* | p.p. of to mine: burrowed in earth; made hole underground. |

| MINER | *n.* | one who works in a mine; soldier whose duty is to lay mines. |
| MINOR | *n.* | person under age. |

| MISSAL | *n.* | book containing service of mass for whole year. |
| MISSEL | *n.* | kind of thrush that feeds on mistletoe berries. |

| MISSED | *v.* | p.p. of to miss: failed to hit mark; failed to find, get or meet. |
| MIST | *n.* | water vapour falling in fine drops smaller than rain. |

MOAN	*n.*	long low murmur of physical or mental suffering.
MOWN	*v.*	p.p. of to mow: cut down grass with scythe or machine.
MOAT	*n.*	deep wide ditch surrounding town or castle, filled with water.
MOTE	*n.*	particle of dust; a trifling fault if compared to one's own.
MODE	*n.*	way or manner in which a thing is done; prevailing fashion.
MOWED	*v.*	p. of to mow: have cut grass.
MOOSE	*n.*	North American animal closely allied to European elk.
MOUSSE	*n.*	dish of various flavours, of cream whipped and frozen, e.g. *chocolate, chestnut mousse.*
MORN	*n.*	morning (poetic); early part of day.
MOURN	*v.*	feel sorrow or regret for dead person, lost thing or misfortune.
MUSCLE	*n.*	one of the contractile fibrous bands that produce movement in animal body.
MUSSEL	*n.*	kind of bivalve mollusc of sea or fresh water.
MUSTARD	*n.*	condiment made from seeds of plant ground down into paste; hot.
MUSTERED	*v.*	p.p. of to muster: collected together a body of men to be checked and inspected.

N

NAVAL	*a.*	pertaining to ships, including the navy.
NAVEL	*n.*	depression in centre of belly after severance of the umbilical cord.
NAVE	*n.*	body of a church running from inner door to chancel or choir.
KNAVE	*n.*	unprincipled man; rogue; lowest court card of each suit in playing cards.

There seems to be a knave in the nave.

NAY	*n.*	negative comment; utter denial or refusal.
NEIGH	*n.*	cry of a horse.
NAZE	*n.*	headland or promontary.
NEIGHS	*v.*	makes a cry of a horse.
NEED	*see*	KNEAD
NEW	*see*	KNEW
NICKS	*n.*	notches made as a guide; incisions.
NIX	*n.*	nothing; also a water elf.

"Night knight."

NIGHT	*n.*	period of darkness between day and day; from 6 p.m. to 6 a.m.; from sunset to sunrise.
KNIGHT	*n.*	one of noble birth who has served as a squire, raised to honourable military rank by king or qualified person.
NIT	*see*	KNIT

NO	*see*	KNOW

NOB	*see*	KNOB

NONE	*pro.*	not any of; no one; no person.
NUN	*n.*	woman living in a convent, under vows of poverty and obedience.

NOR	*see*	GNAW

NOSE	*see*	KNOWS

Not a very good knot.

NOT	*adv.*	word negating what follows.
KNOT	*n.*	intertwining of parts of one or more ropes or strings to fasten them together.

O

OAR	*n.*	pole with blade, used to propel by leverage a boat, worked by a single rower with both hands.
OR	*conj.*	affording alternatives or choices.
	n.	gold or yellow in armorial bearings.
ORE	*n.*	mineral aggregate from which precious or commercially profitable metal can be produced.
O'ER	*adv.*	poetic version of 'over'.
AWE	*n.*	wonder or solemn reaction to spectacle, tinged with fear. Also one of the floatboards of undershot waterwheel.

They came o'er the sea by oar and stood in awe of the ore.

| ODE | n. | poem meant to be sung. |
| OWED | v. | p.p. of to owe: was under an obligation to pay a debt to a person. |

| OH! | int. | expression of surprise and a variety of emotions in different situations. |
| OWE | v. | have a duty to pay money which is due; to be in debt. |

| ONE | n. | single or half of two. |
| WON | v. | p.p. of to win: have been victorious in any attempt either physical or mental. |

| ORAL | a. | spoken; verbal; by word of mouth. |
| AURAL | a. | pertaining to the organ of hearing; received by the ear. |

Oral . . . . . Aural.

OUGHT	*see*	AUGHT
OUR	*see*	HOUR

OVA   *n.*   pl. of ovum: female germ in animals, capable of developing into new individual when fertilized by the male sperm.

OVER   *adv.*   with motion above something so as to pass across something.

          n.   set of six deliveries of the ball in cricket.

P

PACED   *v.*   p.p. of to pace: stepped; measured out by walking.

PASTE   *n.*   flour moistened and kneaded with butter; hard vitreous composition used in making imitation gems; any soft plastic mixture.

He paced in the paste.

PACKED   *v.*   p.p. of to pack: put things together into a bundle, box or bag for transport or storing.

PACT   *n.*   compact; agreement.

PAIL   *n.*   vessel, usually round, of wood or metal for carrying liquids.

PALE   *a.*   of whitish or ashen appearance; faintly coloured.

              n.   one of the upright bars nailed vertically to a horizontal rail to form a paling.

75

PAIN	*n.*	suffering; distress of body or mind; trouble taken; industriousness.
PANE	*n.*	single sheet of glass in compartment of a window; rectangular division of chequered pattern.
PAIR	*n.*	set of two; couple; article consisting of two corresponding parts not used separately.
PARE	*v.*	trim thing by cutting away irregular parts; cut away skin.
PEAR	*n.*	sweet fleshy fruit, tapering towards stalk.
PATIENCE	*n.*	calm endurance of pain or any provocation; perseverance.
PATIENTS	*n.*	pl. persons under medical treatment.

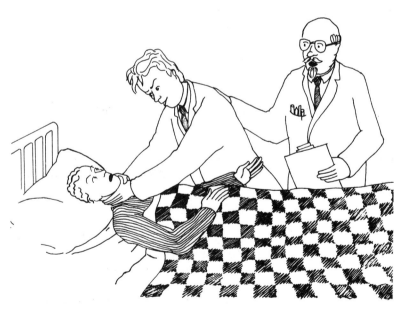

"Really, Doctor! You should have more patience with your patients!"

76

PAUSE	*n.*	interval of inaction or silence; hesitation.
PAWS	*n.*	feet of beasts having claws or nails.
PORES	*n.*	minute openings, esp. in skin of animals, through which fluids may pass.
PAWN	*n.*	thing or person left in another's keeping as pledge, security.
PORN	*n.*	abbreviation of pornography: treatment of obscene subjects in literature.
PEACE	*n.*	freedom from, cessation of war; freedom from civil disorder.
PIECE	*n.*	one of the distinct protions of which a thing is composed.

Peek from a peak.

PEAK	*n.*	projecting part of brim of hat; pointed top esp. of mountain.
PEEK	*n.*	peer (quickly); peep.
PIQUE	*n.*	irritation; wounded pride.

PEAL	*n.*	long ringing of bell; series of 'changes' on set of bells.
PEEL	*v.*	strip rind from orange, skin from potato, or bark from tree.
PEARL	*n.*	concretion, usually white or bluish grey, formed within the shell of pearl oyster or other bivalve, having beautiful lustre; a gem.
PURL	*n.*	ale or beer with wormwood infused; hot beer mixed with gin.

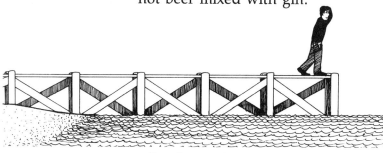

Peer from a pier.

PEER	*n.*	an equal in civil standing or rank; an equal in any respect; a long gaze.
PIER	*n.*	breakwater; mole; structure of iron or wood running out into the sea and used as a promenade or landing stage.
PER	*prep.*	by; by means of; through; instrumentally.
PURR	*v.*	make low vibrating sound of pleasure; utter words of content.

PHALLUSES	*see*	FALLACIES
PHIAL	*see*	FILE
PHILTRE	*see*	FILTER

78

PHIZ	*see*	FIZZ
PHLOX	*see*	FLOCKS
PLACE	*n.*	particular part of space; part of space occupied by a person or thing.
PLAICE	*n.*	European flat fish much used as food.
PLAIN	*a.*	simple; easily understood; in card games those that are not court cards.
	n.	bare stretch of country.
PLANE	*n.*	tall spreading tree with broad leaves; main road in mine; tool for smoothing surface of woodwork.
PLUM	*n.*	fruit, fleshy and rounded with hard stone; best of a bunch; conglomeration of flint and pebbles.
PLUMB	*n.*	sea measure of depth with a plummet; in cricket a level true wicket; just nonsense (fig.).
PSALTER	*n.*	book of Psalms.
SALTER	*n.*	person who salts fish.
PROFIT	*n.*	advantage; benefit; pecuniary gain; excess of returns over outlay.
PROPHET	*n.*	inspired teacher; revealer or interpreter of God's will; one who foretells events.

Q

QUARTS	*n.pl.*	measure of capacity; quarter of a gallon or two pints.
QUARTZ	*n.*	a widely diffused mineral, massive or crystallizing in hexagonal prisms, in a pure form consisting of silica or silicon dioxide.
QUAY	*see*	KEY

Cue the queue.

QUEUE	*n.*	line of persons or vehicles waiting their turn to be attended to or proceed; plaited tail of hair, or wig, hanging down.
CUE	*n.*	last words of dialogue in a play which signal to another actor to speak or enter; long, straight tapering rod for striking ball in billiards.
QUIRE	*see*	CHOIR
QUOIN	*see*	COIN

R

RABBET   *n.*   step-shaped reduction cut along edge of wood etc. usually to receive the edge or tongue of another.

RABBIT   *n.*   burrowing rodent of the hare family, brownish grey in natural state; also black, white or pied in domestication.

RACK   *n.*   fixed or movable frame of wooden or metal bars for holding fodder, or for keeping articles on.

WRACK   *n.*   seaweed cast up and used for manure; wreckage.

RAIN   *n.*   condensed moisture of atmosphere falling visibly in drops.

REIGN   *n.*   sovereignty; rule; sway.

RAISE   *v.*   set upright; make stand up; restore to, or towards vertical.

RAZE   *v.*   wound slightly; graze; completely destroy; level to the ground.

RAP   *n.*   smart, slight blow; punishment inflicted on child; sound made by knocker on door; skein of 120 yards of yarn.

WRAP   *v.*   enfold, enclose, pack or conceal in folded or soft encircling material.

| RAPT | *v.* | p.p. of to rap: snatched away bodily or carried away in spirit from earth, from life, from consciousness or from ordinary thoughts. |
| WRAPPED | *v.* | p.p. of to wrap: enfolded, enclosed or packed in encircling material. |

| RAW | *a.* | uncooked; without scalding (of milk); not hardened by fire. |
| ROAR | *n.* | loud, deep, hoarse sound as of lion, person or company in pain or rage. |

| READ | *v.* | p.p. of to read: interpreted mentally; declared interpretation of written symbols; reproduced mentally or vocally the words of book or letter. |
| RED | *a.* | colour seen at one end of the spectrum in varying shades from crimson to bright brown or orange, especially that seen in sunsets. |

| READ | *v.* | to interpret the meaning and intention of words by studying them. |
| REED | *n.* | kind of firm-stemmed water or marsh plant, used for thatching. |

REAL	*a.*	actually existing as a thing; occurring in fact; objective, genuine; rightly so called; natural; sincere; not artificial.
REEL	*n.*	lively Scottish dance.
	v.	to be dizzy, sway or be in a whirl.

| REEK | *n.* | smoke vapour; visible exhalation; foul or stale odour; fetid atmosphere. |
| WREAK | *v.* | avenge wrong; give satisfaction to; put in operation. |

REST	*n.*	stillness; ceasing exertion; tranquillity; remainder of some quantity or number; reserve fund.
WREST	*v.*	twist; deflect; distort; pervert; force or wrench away from grasp.
RETCH	*v.*	make the motion of vomiting, especially ineffectually or involuntarily.
WRETCH	*n.*	vile, sorry or despicable person.
REVIEW	*v.*	view again; survey; look back on; write a notice of a play.
REVUE	*n.*	loosely linked scenes satirising current events, of a humorous artistic nature.
RIGHT	*a.*	correct, true, straight; of conduct, just; morally good.
RITE	*n.*	form of procedure; action required or usual; religious ceremony.
WRITE	*v.*	trace symbols representing words, with pen or pencil, on paper or parchment; put into literary form; set down in writing.
RIME	*n.*	hoar frost.
RHYME	*n.*	identity of sound between words extending from the end to the last fully accented vowel and not further.
RING	*v.*	give forth clear resonant sound of vibrating metal; announce hour by sound of bells.
WRING	*v.*	squeeze clothes to extract water from them.

ROAD	*n.*	piece of water near shore in which ships can ride at anchor; line of communication between places for use of foot passengers, vehicles etc.
RODE	*v.*	p.p. of to ride: sit on and be carried by horse etc.
ROWED	*v.*	p.p. of to row: convey or propel a boat using oars.
ROC	*n.*	gigantic bird of eastern tales.
ROCK	*n.*	solid part of earth's crust underlying soil.

Roc on a rock.

ROES	*n.*	pl. mass of eggs in fish's ovarian membrane, liked as food.
ROSE	*n.*	beautiful prickly shrub bearing fragrant flowers of red, white or yellow colour.
ROWS	*n.*	pl. numbers of persons or things in more or less straight lines.
RÔLE	*n.*	actor's part; one's function; what one was appointed to do.
ROLL	*n.*	cylinder formed by turning flexible fabric over and over on itself without folding.

"He can't believe he's had to stoop to the rôle of a roll."

ROOD	*n.*	quarter of an acre, a small piece of land; cross of Christ.
RUDE	*a.*	primitive; simple; unsophisticated; uncivilized; coarse.
ROOT	*n.*	part of a plant normally below earth's surface, and serving to attach it to earth and convey nourishment from soil to it.
ROUTE	*n.*	way taken in getting from starting point to destination.

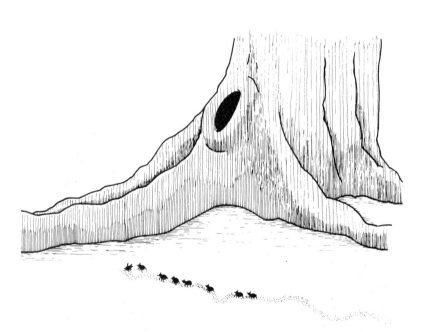

"There seems to be a large root blocking our route."

ROTE	*n.*	mere habituation; repetition.
WROTE	*v.*	p.p. of to write: put down in writing.
ROUGH	*a.*	of uneven or irregular surface; not smooth or level.
RUFF	*n.*	neck piece of deep projecting frill of linen, or muslin, starched and goffered; small fresh water fish; bird of sandpiper kind; trump in card game.

"Your rows have made me rouse myself."

ROUSE	*v.*	startle game from lair or cover; waken up; stir from sleep.
ROWS	*n.pl.*	disturbance; commotions; noises; disputes.
ROUX	*n.*	mixture of melted butter and flour used for thickening soups and gravies.
RUE	*n.*	perennial evergreen shrub with bitter strong-scented leaves.
RYE	*n.*	grain of north European cereal used for bread in northern Continental countries.
WRY	*a.*	distorted; turned to one side; skew; ironical.

S

SAIL	*n.*	piece of canvas or other textile extended on rigging to catch wind and propel vessel.
SALE	*n.*	exchange of a commodity for money or other valuable commodity.
SALTER	*see*	PSALTER
SAUCE	*n.*	liquid in preparation taken as relish with some articles of food; cheekiness.
SOURCE	*n.*	spring, fountain head from which stream issues; material essential to writing of history and other literary subjects.
SAW	*n.*	implement, usually of steel, with blade having teeth for dividing wood metal or stone.
SOAR	*v.*	fly high; be at a great height above the earth; hover in the air without flapping wings.
SORE	*a.*	tender; bruised; inflamed; afflicted.
SAWED	*v.*	p.p. of to saw: cut wood with a saw.
SWORD	*n.*	offensive weapon consisting of long, variously shaped blade for cutting and thrusting with hilt and handguard.

| SCENE | *n.* | place on which something is exhibited or drama is set forth; portion of a play in which action may be continuous. |
| SEEN | *v.* | p.p. of to see: discerned objects with the eye. |

| SCENT | *see* | CENT |

| SENSE | *see* | CENTS |

| SCULL | *v.* | kind of boat propelled by oars. |
| SKULL | *n.* | bony case of the brain; frame of the head; cranium. |

| SEA | *n.* | expanse of salt water that covers most of the earth's surface. |
| SEE | *v.* | to discern with the eye. |

"See the sea and the sun, son." (see also p.95)

89

SEAM	*n.*	line of junction between two edges, especially that of two pieces of cloth, turned back and sewn together.
SEEM	*v.*	have the air, appearance or sensation of being; apparently perceived.
SEAMEN	*n.*	men who follow an occupation connected with the sea.
SEMEN	*n.*	generative fluid of male animals; seed.
SEAR	*n.*	catch of gunlock holding hammer at half or full-cock.
SEER	*n.*	prophet; person who sees visions; one with preternatural sight.

"Right, men! Let's seize the seas!"

SEAS	*n.*	pl. of sea, which see.
SEIZE	*v.*	take possession of by warrant or legal right; lay hold of forcibly, snatch; grasp with hand or mind.
SEED	*see*	CEDE
SEEK	*v.*	make search or enquiry for; be anxious to find thing; aim at.
SIKH	*n.*	member of religious sect founded in Punjab.

"Seeing as you're getting out next week, sell us your half of the cell."

| SELL | *v.* | make over or exchange for money; barter. |
| CELL | *n.* | single person's small room in monastery or prison. |

| SELLER | *see* | CELLAR |

| SERF | *n.* | villein; person whose service is attached to the soil; drudge. |
| SURF | *n.* | foam and commotion of sea breaking on shore or reefs. |

| SERGE | *n.* | kind of double-twilled worsted fabric used mostly for rough wear. |
| SURGE | *n.* | movement up and down and to and fro as in waves of sea. |

SEW	*v.*	fasten materials by passing thread again and again through holes made with threaded needle or awl.
SO	*conj.*	to the extent; in the manner set forth; definite but unspecified sum; exclamatory emphasis.
SOW	*v.*	scatter seed on or in earth for purpose of growth.
SHAKE	*v.*	move violently up or down, to and fro.
SHEIK	*n.*	chief, head of Arabian tribe, family, village or country.

"That sheik sure can shake!"

| SHEAR | v. | cut with a sword; clip; cut with scissors or shears; reduce nap by doing so. |
| SHEER | adv. | mere; simple; unassisted; undiluted; uncompounded; neither more nor less than. |

| SHIRE | n. | county (many counties take the suffix 'shire', but some not), Leicestershire, what was Rutland and Huntingdon are generally known as the hunting shires. |
| SHYER | a. | more shy than another. |

"Shoo! Shoo! Giant shoe!"

| SHOE | n | outer foot covering, not reaching above the ankle. |
| SHOO | int. | sound used to frighten birds away. |

| SHOOT | v. | discharge bullet from a gun; kill or wound with missile from a gun. |
| SHUTE | n. | channel or open trough for conveying water to a lower level, or ore, coal or grain similarly. |

"The way the other side sighed when we won!"

SIDE	*n.*	one of the flat surfaces bounding an object.
SIGHED	*v.*	p.p. of to sigh: drew deep, audible breaths expressive of sadness.
SIGHS	*n.pl.*	deep breaths expressive of weariness, relief from tension, cessation of effort.
SIZE		standard of weight or measure for some article; dimension; magnitude.
SIGHT	*see*	CITE
SIGN	*n.*	mark traced on surface; fanciful device painted on board, displayed formerly by traders, inns or barbers.
SINE	*n.*	ratio in trigonometry.
SYNE	*adv.*	Scottish form of 'since'; days of long ago; especially as in a song sung at parting, '*Auld Lang Syne.*'

SITE	*see*	CITE
SLAY	*v.*	kill.
SLEIGH	*n.*	vehicle on runners instead of wheels, for going over snow, drawn by horses or dogs.
SLEIGHT	*n.*	dexterity; cunning; deceptive trick; quickness of hand in fencing; legerdemain.
SLIGHT	*a.*	slender; slim; frail; inconsiderable.
SLOE	*n.*	small bluish-black fruit like a wild plum.
SLOW	*adv.*	not quick; deficient in speed.
SOLD	*v.*	p.p. of to sell, which see.
SOLED	*v.*	p.p. of to sole: provided shoe with leather or material foundation.
SOLE	*n.*	kind of flat fish much esteemed as food.
SOUL	*n.*	the immaterial part of man, moral or emotional.
SOME	*adj.*	particular, but unknown or unspecified.
SUM	*n.*	total amount resulting from addition of items.
SON	*n.*	male child of a parent.
SUN	*n.*	the heavenly body that the earth travels round and recieves warmth or light from, or both.
SOUGH	*v.*	make moaning, rushing or whistling sound as of wind in trees.
SOW	*n.*	adult female pig.

SOUGHT	*v.*	p.p. of to seek: looked for; searched for.
SORT	*n.*	group of things with common attributes; class; kind; species.
SOURCE	*see*	SAUCE
SPA	*n.*	place where there is a mineral spring.
SPAR	*n.*	stout pole such as is used for the mast of a ship.
STAID	*a.*	of steady or sober character; sedate.
STAYED	*v.*	p.p. of to stay; checked; stopped; appeased hunger temporarily; postponed.
STAIR	*n.*	each of a set of steps from one landing to another, used by servants and others mounting to floors above.
STARE	*n.*	look fixedly with the eyes open with surprise or admiration.

Find the source of this sauce.

How not to stalk a stork.

STALK	*v.*	stride; walk in a stately or imposing manner; hunt pursue game warily.
STORK	*n.*	tall stately wading bird allied to heron.
STATIONARY	*a.*	remaining in one place; not moving; not changing.
STATIONERY	*n.*	writing materials supplied by stationer.
STAKE	*n.*	stick sharpened at one end and driven into the ground for support; money wagered on an event.
STEAK	*n.*	slice of beef, pork, venison or fish cut for broiling, roasting on a spit or frying.

STEAL	*v.*	take away secretly for one's own use, without right or leave; take feloniously; get possession of by insidious arts.
STEEL	*n.*	metal used for tools, weapons, knives etc.
STILE	*n.*	step or some provision other than a gate enabling people to get over a fence.
STYLE	*n.*	manner of doing as opposed to matter; way of expression.
STOREY	*n.*	any of the parts into which a house is divided horizontally.
STORY	*n.*	account given of an incident or a life; narrative; main facts or plot of novel, epic or play.
STOOP	*v.*	bring one's head nearer the ground by bending down from a standing position; lower oneself.
STOUP	*n.*	flagon; beaker; drinking vessel; holy water basin.
STRAIGHT	*a.*	without curve or bend; extending uniformly in one direction; not crooked.
STRAIT	*n.*	narrow passage of water connecting two seas.
SUCCOUR	*v.*	come to the assistance of; give aid to.
SUCKER	*n.*	person or thing that sucks: sucking pig, new born whale; person of immature mind; greenhorn (coll.).

SUEDE	*n.*	undressed kid as used for gloves or shoes.
SWAYED	*v.*	p.p. of to sway: leaned unsteadily from side to side; moved with a swinging motion; persuaded; influenced.
SUITE	*n.*	retinue, persons in attendance on someone; musical succession of movements in dance style.
SWEET	*a.*	tasting like sugar or honey; fragrant; agreeable.
SWAT	*v.*	slap; crush (a fly).
SWOT	*v.*	study hard at books; get up a subject hurriedly.

T

TACKED	*v.*	p.p. of to tack: secure a carpet with flat-headed nails; temporary stitching in needlework.
TACT	*n.*	intuitive perception of what is fitting; adroitness in dealing with persons or circumstances.
TAIL	*n.*	hindermost part of an animal when prolonged beyond the rest of the body.
TALE	*n.*	imaginative narrative; story; malicious report.
TALK	*v.*	converse; communicate ideas by spoken words, or by wireless signals.
TORQUE	*n.*	necklace of twisted metal worn by Gauls.
TARE	*n.*	common vetch, a plant; allowance made for weight of box in which goods are packed.
TEAR	*v.*	pull violently apart; rend asunder with force.
TAUGHT	*v.*	p.p. of to teach: enabled a person, by instruction and training, to learn a trade or profession.
TAUT	*a.*	tight; not slack.

..... so they had tea on the tee. (see CADDIE)

TEA	*n.*	shrub or small tree of the camellia family grown in Ceylon and China and other countries whose leaves are dried for use as a beverage.
TEE	*n.*	cleared space from which a golf-ball is struck at the start of play for each hole.
TEAM	*n.*	two or more beasts of burden harnessed together; set of players on each side in a football or other game.
TEEM	*v.*	bear offspring; be prolific; be stocked to overflowing.
TEAR	*n.*	drop of saline liquid ordinarily serving to wash the eye but falling from it as a result of grief or other emotion.
TIER	*n.*	row or rank of seats or other things, especially one of several placed one above another as in a theatre.

TEASE	*v.*	assail playfully or maliciously; vex with questions, jests or petty annoyances; to card cloth with teasels.
TEES	*n.pl.*	umbrella-shaped gilded ornaments crowning a pagoda.
TENNER	*n.*	coll. ten pound money note.
TENOR	*n.*	singer with highest ordinary adult male voice, between baritone and alto.
TERN	*n.*	seabird like a gull.
TURN	*v.*	move on an axis; convey rotary motion to; change from one side to another.

"They're there with their friend."

THEIR	*adj.*	possessive case of they.
THERE	*adv.*	in that place; in one's senses; sane.
THEY'RE	*n. & v.*	they are.

THREW	*v.*	p.p. of to throw: flung violently, cast away.
THROUGH	*prep.*	from end to end of; side to side of; train going all the way without change of line.
THROW	*n.*	cast of fishing line or dice; distance a missile is thrown;
THROE	*n.*	violent pang as of childbirth; anguish (usually pl.).
THRONE	*n.*	chair of state for sovereign or bishop, usually decorated and raised on dais.
THROWN	*v.*	p.p. of to throw: released a ball after imparting motion; propelled through space; dismissed with some violence; flung, hurled.

"He should be thrown from the throne!"

103

TIC	*n.*	habitual spasmodic contraction of muscles of the face.
TICK	*n.*	stout usually striped linen or cotton material used for cover for bedding.
TIDE	*n.*	periodical rise and fall of sea due to attraction of moon and sun.
TIED	*v.*	p.p. of to tie: attached; fastened; came to an equal score or dead heat in a game.
TIME	*n.*	conditions of life, prevailing circumstances of a period.
THYME	*n.*	shrub with pungent aromatic leaves used in cookery.
TIRE	*v.*	make or grow weary; to have had enough of a thing.
TYRE	*n.*	band of metal or rubber placed round rim of a wheel to strengthen or prevent jar.
TO	*adv.*	in the direction of.
TOO	*adv.*	higher than admissible; more than should be; as well as.
TWO	*n.*	one more than one; 'two-step' — a kind of round dance.
TOAD	*n.*	amphibian like a frog but with clumsy and warty body.
TOWED	*v.*	p.p. of to tow: pulled a boat, barge or vehicle along behind one.
TOE	*n.*	digit of the foot; fore part of hoof.
TOW	*v.*	pull a thing along behind one; drag net over surface to collect specimen.

TRUSSED	*v.*	p.p. of to truss: having its wings fastened before cooking, of a fowl; having arms tied to sides, of a person.
TRUST	*n.*	confidence reposed in one.
TUBA	*n.*	bass brass instrument of large size.
TUBER	*n.*	short thick part of underground stem of a plant: potato, artichoke or dahlia.

U

URN	*see*	EARN
USE	*v.*	employ for a purpose; handle an instrument; exercise.
EWES	*n.pl.*	female sheep.
YEWS	*n.pl.*	slow growing, dark-leaved, evergreen tree, often planted in graveyards and used for making bows.

I see you use ewes to pull down your yews.

V

VAIN	*a.*	unsubstantial; empty; trivial; unavailing.
VANE	*n.*	weathercock.
VEIN	*n.*	each of the membranous tubes that convey blood to the heart; blood vessel.
VALE	*n.*	valley.
VEIL	*n.*	piece of transparent material attached to a woman's bonnet to conceal her face.
VAULT	*n.*	arched roof; arched cellar or subterranean chamber as place of storage.
VOLT	*n.*	unit of electromotive force.

"If they break into either of these vaults they'll get 10,000 volts."

"Get rid of that vile viol player with this vial."

VIAL	*n.*	small glass vessel for holding liquid medicines.
VILE	*a.*	worthless; morally base; depraved.
VIOL	*n.*	baroque stringed musical instrument, predecessor of the violin.
		also see FILE and PHIAL.

W

WADE	*v.*	walk through water or other impeding medium such as snow, mud or sand; read a book in spite of dullness.
WEIGHED	*v.*	p.p. of to weigh: measured with scales or other machine; balanced in hands as if to guess weight.
WAIL	*n.*	prolonged, high-pitched, plaintive, inarticulate cry; Jews be*wail* the destruction of the Temple at the Wailing Wall.
WHALE	*n.*	large fish-like mammal.

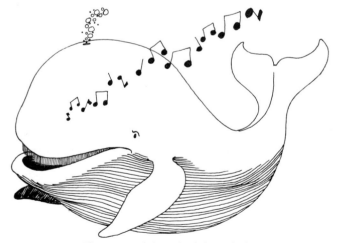

The mournful wail of the whale.

109

A wain train wanes.

WAIN   *n.*   wagon, chiefly poetical or agricultural.
WANE   *v.*   decrease in size or splendour like the
                moon after the full.

"We appear to be up to the waist in waste.

WAIST	*n.*	part of the human body below ribs and above hips.
WASTE	*n.*	desert; dreary scene; useless remains.
WAIT	*v.*	abstain from action or departure until some expected event occurs; pause; tarry; stay; kick one's heels.
WEIGHT	*n.*	heaviness; burden of load.
WAIVE	*v.*	forbear to insist on.
WAVE	*n.*	long body of water curling into arched form and breaking on shore.
WAR	*n.*	quarrel between nations conducted by force; state of open hostility.
WORE	*v.*	past tense of to wear: dressed habitually in.
WARE	*n.*	article manufactured for sale.
WEAR	*v.*	dress habitually in; endure continued use.
WHERE	*n.*	place; scene of something.

111

WARN	v.	give notice to; put on guard; admonish of danger.
WORN	v.	p.p. of to wear: tired, of used aspect; frayed; not new.

WATT	n.	unit of electrical power.
WHAT	a.	asking for selection from an indefinite number of.

WAY	n.	road or track provided for passing along.
WEIGH	v.	find weight of.
WHEY	n.	part that remains liquid when sour milk forms curds.

WAX	n.	sticky, plastic, yellowish substance secreted by bees for honeycomb cells.
WHACKS	n.pl.	heavy blows with a stick.

WEAK	a.	wanting in strength; fragile; easily broken; not strong.
WEEK	n.	period of seven days.

WEAL	n.	ridge raised on person's flesh by stroke of rod or whip.
WHEEL	n.	circular frame or disc arranged to revolve on axis and used to facilitate motion of a vehicle.

WEATHER	n.	atmospheric conditions prevailing at a place or time.
WHETHER	n.	castrated ram.

WIER	n.	dam across a river, to raise level of water above it; enclosure of stakes set in stream as trap for fish.
WE'RE	n. & v.	abbreviation of 'we are'.

WELD	*v.*	unite into a homogenous mass by hammering (of metal).
WELLED	*v.*	p.p. of to well: spring forth as from a fountain.
WET	*a.*	soaked, covered, dabbled, moistened or supplied with water.
WHET	*v.*	sharpen by rubbing on a stone; stimulate appetite.
WHICH	*a.*	interrogative adjective asking for selection from alternatives.
WITCH	*n.*	woman practicing sorcery; fascinating, bewitching woman; ugly old woman; hag.
WHILED	*v.*	p.p. of to while: passed the time away; let slip by leisurely.
WILD	*a.*	not domesticated or cultivated.
WHILE	*conj.*	during the time that; for as long as.
WILE	*n.*	trick; cunning procedure; artifice.
WHINE	*v.*	make long drawn complaining cry; utter querulous talk.
WINE	*n.*	fermented grape juice; a drink fit for gods.
WHIRLED	*v.*	p.p. of to whirl: swung round and round; revolved rapidly.
WORLD	*n.*	the earth, its countries and their inhabitants.

Meanwhile the world whirled.

113

"You've only a whit of wit."

WHIT	*n.*	particle; least possible amount.
WIT	*n.*	intelligence; understanding: power of giving sudden intellectual pleasure by unexpected combination of ideas.

WHITHER	*adv.*	interrogative adverb: to what place, point or destination?
WITHER	*v.*	become dry or shrivelled; lose vigour vitality or freshness.

WHOLE	*see*	HOLE

WHORE	*see*	HOAR

WON	*see*	ONE

WOOD	*n.*	growing trees occupying considerable tract of land; fibrous substance between pith and bark of trees.
WOULD	*v.*	want; desire; choose.
WRACK	*see*	RACK
WRAP	*see*	RAP
WREAK	*see*	REEK
WREST	*see*	REST
WRING	*see*	RING
WRITE	*see*	RIGHT
WROTE	*see*	ROTE
WRY	*see*	RYE

Y

YAWS	*n.pl.*	framboesis.
YOURS	*pro.*	of or belonging to you.
YEW	*n.*	wood of kind of slow growing dark leaved evergreen tree often planted in graveyards.
YOU	*pro.*	second person pronoun, singular and plural: the person addressed.
EWE	*n.*	female sheep.
YEWS	*see*	USE
YOKE	*n.*	wooden cross-piece over necks of two oxen, attached to plough or wagon that they are to draw.
YOLK	*n.*	yellow part of egg.
YORE	*n.*	formerly; of old days.
YOUR	*a.*	of you; belonging to you.
YOU'RE	*n. & v.*	abbreviation of 'you are'.

Ewe by a yew.